The Long E

Story by Jackie Tidey
Photography by Lindsay Edwards

Rigby
A Harcourt Achieve Imprint

www.Rigby.com
1-800-531-5015

"Dad!" shouted Jake.
"Can you see the car ferry?"

"Yes," said Dad,
"it's going to the big dock
where we went fishing."

"Can we go and see it?"
said Jake.

"Yes, we can," said Dad,
"but the dock is a long way
from here.
It will be a long ride."

"I'm a good rider," said Jake.
"I can ride all the way
to the dock."

Dad and Jake went down the path
by the beach.

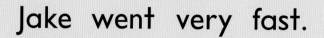

Jake went very fast.

"Jake, you are going too fast," shouted Dad.

"Slow down!

Stay with me!"

8

"But we will not see the cars
coming out of the ferry," said Jake.

"Yes, we will," said Dad.
"The ferry is going slowly."

At last they got to the big dock.

"Dad," said Jake,
"the door of the ferry is open.
Have all the cars and trucks
come out?"

"No," said Dad, "here they come."

They looked at the cars
and trucks coming slowly
out of the ferry.

"I'm very hot
after that long bike ride," said Jake.

"Let's get some ice cream," said Dad.

"This is good," laughed Jake.